CHAMPS!

INSPIRATIONAL ANIMALS

Brave Birds

Cherry Lake Press
Ann Arbor, Michigan

by Joyce Markovics

CHERRY LAKE PRESS

Published in the United States of America by Cherry Lake Publishing
Ann Arbor, Michigan
www.cherrylakepublishing.com

Reading Adviser: Beth Walker Gambro, MS, Ed., Reading Consultant, Yorkville, IL
Content Adviser: William Tavolacci, LVT, CCRP Team Leader, Integrative and Rehabilitative Medicine Department, Schwarzman Animal Medical Center

Book Designer: Ed Morgan
Book Developer: Bowerbird Books

Photo Credits: © Werner Baumgarten/Shutterstock, cover and title page; © Ivonne Wierink/Shutterstock, 5; © Candice Coghlin/Shutterstock, 6; © Walkin' Pets, 7; © ARTFULLY PHOTOGRAPHER/Shutterstock, 9; © Nitin Chandra/Shutterstock, 10 top; © Eric Isselee/Shutterstock, 10 bottom; © AmyAlyssa/Shutterstock, 11; © Julian Popov/Shutterstock, 13; © Patrick Wood, 15; freepik.com, 16; © Josef Kral/Shutterstock, 17; © Vaclav Matous/Shutterstock, 19; © Walkin' Pets, 20; © janko.knops/Shutterstock, 21.

Cherry Lake Press is an imprint of Cherry Lake Publishing Group.

Library of Congress Cataloging-in-Publication Data has been filed and is available at catalog.loc.gov.

Printed in the United States of America

Note from publisher: Websites change regularly, and their future contents are outside of our control. Supervise children when conducting any recommended online searches for extended learning opportunities.

Contents

Small but MIGHTY

Granite the bantam chicken is one brave bird. She was born with a **deformed** leg. As a result, Granite can't walk. But the tiny chicken hasn't let her **disability** stop her. To get around, she hops on one leg or flies. Her will to live even saved her life. One night, she fought off a weasel all by herself! After the **ordeal**, her owners kept her inside to heal. "If any animal deserves a second chance, this chicken does," said Sarah Wood, one of Granite's owners.

There are different colors and types of bantam chickens.

Bantams are the smallest breed of chicken. They weigh about as much as a pair of sneakers!

Very soon, Granite became part of the family. The chicken even won over the family dog! "She is just so sweet," said Sarah's daughter, Alora. But Granite's human family wanted her to have more **independence**.

Chickens can make loving pets.

That's when Walkin' Pets got involved. The company made a special wheelchair for the chicken. For the first time ever, Granite was able to walk. "It's really improved her quality of life," Alora said. She is inspired by Granite every day. "I just think she's a really great teacher," said Alora.

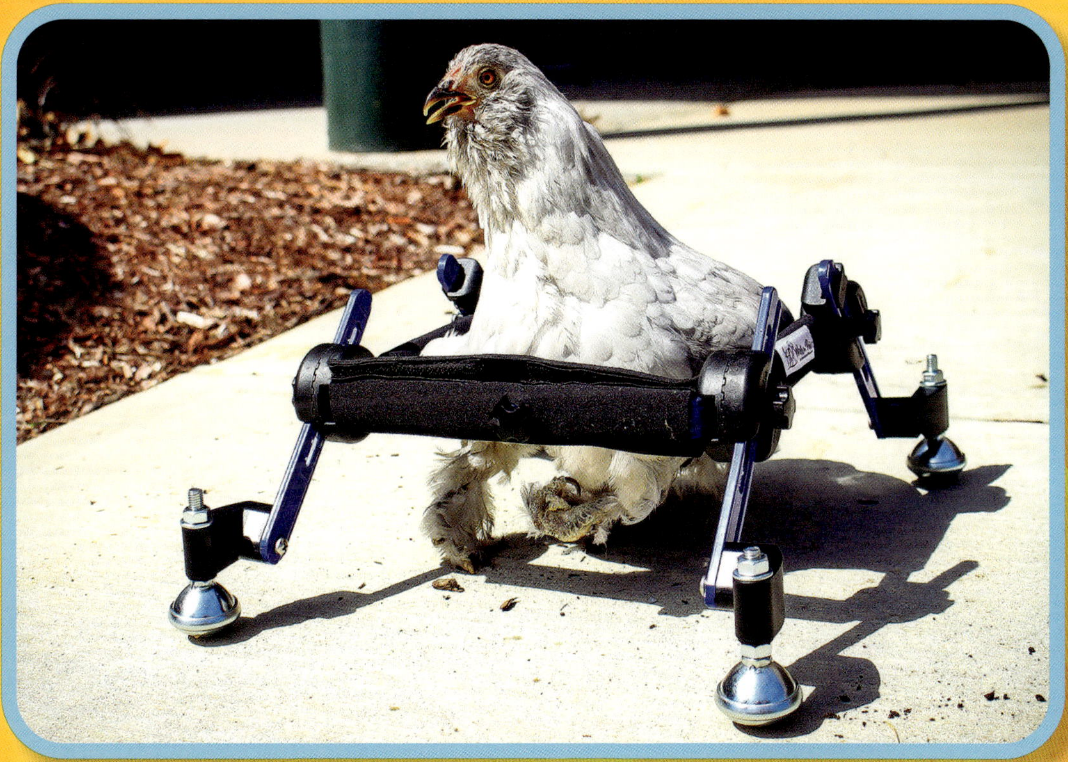

Granite the chicken has the perfect middle name—"Heart."

Walkin' Pets builds wheelchairs and other **mobility aids** for pets. Their wheelchair for Granite was the first of its kind for a chicken!

Extra SPECIAL BIRDS

Disabilities can affect chickens like Granite and other birds. Some disabilities are present from birth. Others can result from an illness or injury. Having a disability can make it hard to do certain things. These things can include walking, hearing, seeing, and learning.

In the past, disabled birds didn't often survive or were **euthanized**. However, today there are many ways to care for them. Humans can help birds with disabilities live full lives. And the birds bring their caregivers lots of joy!

A physical disability affects the body. A mental disability **impacts** the brain or mind.

A broken wing can often be treated.

When Mumble, a rose-ringed parakeet, was born, something was wrong. The baby bird couldn't stand or walk. Yassin Elmahgoub felt called to help. As a medical student, he knew Mumble needed special care. And Yassin was just the person for the job.

In the wild, rose-ringed parakeets live in India and Africa. They're kept as pets around the world.

A rose-ringed parakeet chick

Yassin became Mumble's **surrogate** mother. "I bottle-fed him and started his treatment," he said. Yassin made tiny braces for Mumble's legs. Yassin even sang to the little bird at night. Vets didn't think the parakeet would ever walk. But Yassin believed it was possible.

Yassin never gave up on Mumble. He lovingly cared for the bird. Over time, the parakeet got bigger and stronger. Yassin decided it was time to remove the leg braces. Then the unbelievable happened. Mumble took his first shaky step! Yassin jumped up and down and cried. “All it takes is one person to save a life,” said Yassin. When asked if he would help another disabled bird, Yassin said, “In a heartbeat.”

A rose-ringed parakeet eats out of its owner's hand.

Yassin took a video of Mumble walking for the first time. It has been viewed millions of times!

One Smart PARROT

Bruce the parrot was another bird who beat the odds. When Bruce was a young bird, he lost the top part of his beak. Birds use their beaks to **preen** their feathers. So, Bruce found the perfect solution—a pebble! First, Bruce found a flat pebble. Then using his lower beak and tongue, Bruce grasped it. Finally, he rubbed the pebble against his feathers to clean them. It's as if Bruce made his own **prosthetic** beak!

Bruce is a type of large parrot called a kea. In the wild, keas make their homes in New Zealand.

Bruce's keepers were amazed. The parrot learned the pebble trick all on his own. He also figured out how to eat hard food. This isn't easy with a broken beak. Someone suggested getting Bruce a real prosthetic beak. "He doesn't need one," said the same keeper. "He's fine with his own!" Bruce has taught the people around him an important lesson. "We can learn a lot if we pay a little more attention to what animals are doing," said his keeper.

Keas eat a wide range of foods, including leaves, fruit, and seeds.

Keas are endangered. Only a few thousand remain in the wild.

Parrots live for a very long time. Some of the oldest can live more than 100 years!

To the Rescue!

It takes very special people to care for disabled birds. A lot of them work at rescue organizations. Mickaboo is one of these groups in California. Their motto is, “Every Bird Gets an Equal Chance.” **Volunteers** at Mickaboo care for dozens of special needs birds.

Some of the birds, like April the conure, once flew freely in a flock in San Francisco. After a head injury, April came to Mickaboo. Over time, she got better. But April still has issues from her old injury. Despite this, she is full of life—and love. Her best friend is another disabled conure named Lyon!

Cherry-headed conures are known for a patch of red feathers on their head.

April is a cherry-headed conure, a type of parakeet from South America. No one knows how the conures ended up living freely in San Francisco.

Merlin the rescue duck also has a best friend. Her name is Gigi. And she's a sheep! Merlin was born with a leg problem, leaving him unable to walk. A rescue group, Goats of Anarchy, took him under their wing. The group mostly rescues goats and other hoofed animals. But Merlin needed their help.

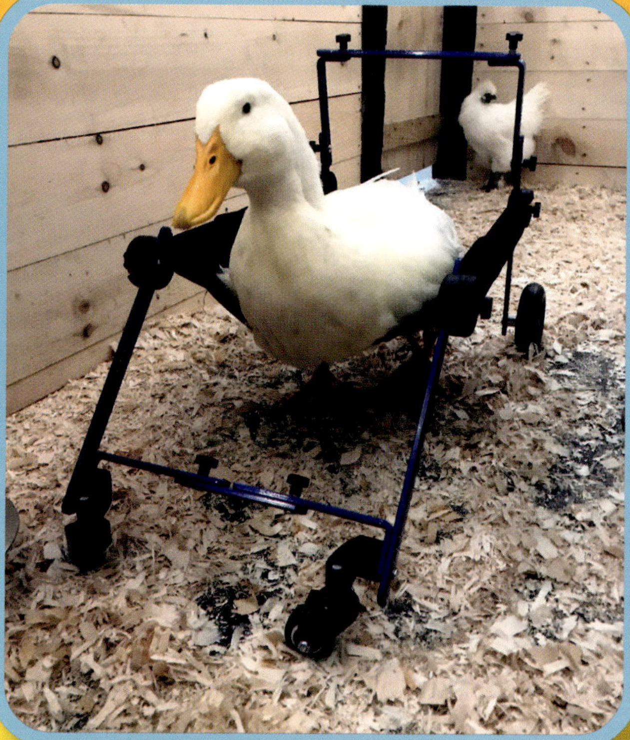

Merlin uses a wheelchair for the first time.

Walkin' Pets found out about Merlin and wanted to help. So, they made the duck a custom wheelchair!

Part of Merlin's daily **therapy** is swimming. After swimming, he rests on the grass. One day, Gigi the sheep stretched out beside him. The cuddle session continued. "Every day, Gigi visits Merlin out in the grass and curls up next to him," said the group's founder. "This relationship is very special."

Merlin loves napping in the sun, especially with Gigi!

Adopting a DISABLED Animal

Animals with disabilities aren't often adopted. Here are some reasons to welcome a disabled animal into your home!

- **Save Lives**
  Because of their special needs, disabled animals are more likely to be euthanized in shelters. Pet adoption can save lives.

- **Companionship**
  Disabled animals provide companionship. They can form very close bonds with their human caregivers.

- **Special Abilities**
  Animals with disabilities can have hidden strengths. For example, a blind animal may have enhanced senses of hearing and smell.

- **Inspire Others**
  Adopting a disabled animal might inspire someone else to do the same!

Glossary

deformed (dih-FORMD) misshapen

disability (diss-uh-BIL-uh-tee) a condition that makes it hard to do certain things, such as walking, seeing, or hearing

euthanized (YOO-thuh-nyezd) painlessly ended the life of a suffering animal

impacts (IM-pakts) strongly affects something

independence (in-duh-PEN-duhns) being able to do things on one's own

mobility aids (mo-BIH-luh-tee AYDZ) tools that help an animal or person move

ordeal (or-DEEL) a difficult experience

preen (PREEN) when a birds cleans its feathers with its beak or tongue

prosthetic (pross-THET-ik) an artificial device that replaces a missing body part

surrogate (SIR-uh-guht) someone or something that replaces something else

therapy (THER-uh-pee) treatments that enhance an animal's abilities and quality of life

volunteers (vol-uhn-TEERZ) people who help others for no pay

Find Out More

BOOKS

125 Animals That Changed the World. Washington, DC: National Geographic Kids, 2019.

Caughey, Melissa. *A Kid's Guide to Keeping Chickens*. New York, NY: Storey Publishing Group, 2015.

Hughes, Catherine D. *Little Kids First Big Book of Birds*. Washington, DC: National Geographic, 2016.

WEBSITES

Explore these online sources with an adult:

Britannica Kids: Bird

Dodo Kids—This Pigeon Loves to Sit on a Puppy!

Mickaboo Companion Bird Rescue

Index

About the Author

Joyce Markovics is passionate about books and animals. She would like to thank Bill Tavolacci and Walkin' Pets for helping disabled animals live fuller, happier lives.